S.S.R.I. would like to thank you for your co-operation during the year.

Inishowen

Paintings & Stories from the land of Eoghan

Paintings by Ros Harvey
Text by Seán Beattie & Martin Lynch

Cottage
Publications

First published by Cottage Publications,
Donaghadee, N. Ireland 2000.
Copyrights Reserved.
© Illustrations by Ros Harvey 2000.
© Text by Seán Beattie & Martin Lynch 2000.

Design & origination in Northern Ireland.
Printed & bound in Singapore.

ISBN 1 900935 17 1

Seán Beattie

Seán Beattie now lives and works as a Guidance Counsellor in Inishowen having studied History and Languages and Education in both Dublin and Coleraine.

He is the author of 'Ancient Monuments of Inishowen' and in addition to editing a heritage guide to Donegal and a poetry anthology, he is a regular contributor on historical topics to the 'Donegal Annual'.

Ros Harvey

Ros Harvey spent her childhood in Malin, and after years working in Dublin and England as a pioneer potter and illustrator has returned and set up the Ballagh Studio from where she continues her painting and print-making.

She works in many mediums her favourite being the soft pastels from which she creates her dramatic landscapes and seascapes, capturing the wild beauty of this most northerly peninsula of Ireland.

Martin Lynch

Also a native of Inishowen, Martin Lynch studied Irish History and Politics. He has taught for many years as well as being a familiar face in the Bookworm Bookshop in Derry.

A keen local historian, Martin is now venturing into the cultural heritage and tourism business in Inishowen and Derry as well as the USA.

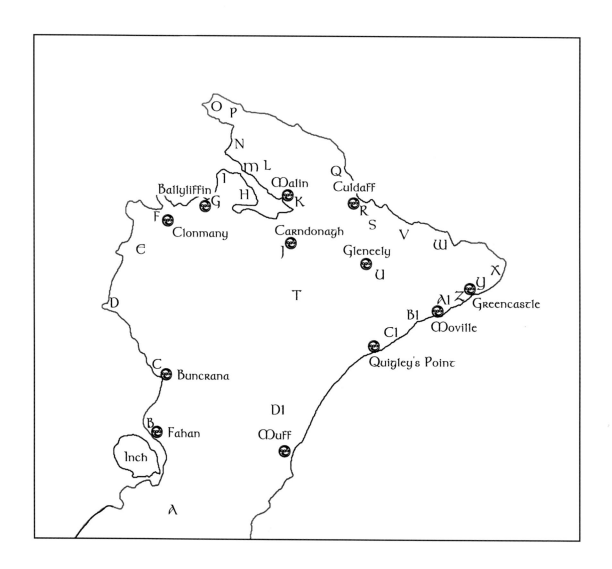

O P
N
m L
l Q
Ballyliffin H Malin Culdaff
G K
F R
Clonmany S
Carndonagh V
E Gleneely W
J
U
X
T
Y
A1 Z
B1 Greencastle
C1
Moville
C
Buncrana Quigley's Point
D
B
Fahan
Inch D1
Muff
A

Contents

Beginnings

Inishowen, in Co. Donegal can be described as Ireland's most northerly peninsula with Malin Head at the North, washed by the Atlantic Ocean. It is bounded by two loughs, the Foyle and the Swilly. The soaring eminence of Slieve Sneacht (the snow mountain) at its centre, gives spectacular views of four counties, Donegal, Tyrone, Derry and Antrim.

The Southern boundary is less well defined. A geographic line of division can be traced from Derry City to Burnfoot, within sight of the historic hill-fort of Grianán Aileach. Historically, it extended along a line from Manorcunningham to Carrigans, but the boundary is unclear.

In shape, it resembles an upside down triangle, lying between 55 degrees and 55.5 degrees North in latitude. It is about 45 kilometres at its widest point and is about 50 kilometres in length from North to South covering an area of 800 square kilometres. Tory Island can be seen from Malin Head and the Scottish islands of Jura and Islay are visible on the skyline, about 60 kilometres across the North Channel.

At the end of the Ice Age, sea levels rose quickly due to the massive melt water from the disintegrating sheets of ice. This water cut across the peninsula at Malin Town, Portmore in Malin Head, the Isle of Doagh and at Burnfoot. In the Burnfoot area, for a time, this had the effect of turning Inishowen into an island. As the weight of ice was lifted from the mainland, and land mass began to rise, the rise in land levels outpaced the rise in the water. The peninsula's name partly derives from this geological period as 'Inish' means Island. The second part of the name dates from the 5th century AD when the peninsula came under the control of Eoghan one of the Uí Néill dynasty.

Geology

God bless the grey mountains
Of dark Donegal.
God bless royal Aileach
The pride of them all.

Beginnings

From the royal hill-fort at Grianán Aileach, the mountains and valleys of Inishowen appear in all their splendour and majesty, the Loughs Foyle and Swilly can clearly be seen. The Swilly is best described as a deep fjord, caused by erosion and it is flanked by steep rocks of quartzite. The Foyle has a different geological structure. It has a wider expanse of water which is quite shallow in places with carboniferous rocks in evidence.

The waters of the Swilly reflect the craggy hills of Knockalla, known as "the Devil's Backbone" and the gnarled uneven hills of Urris. The name "Lake of Shadows" is very appropriate, especially on a calm summer evening. The deepest part of the Swilly is between Fanad shore and Dunree Head, and here it shows evidence of overdeepening. With the rise in the sea-level in post-glacial times, a submerged sill was deposited at the entrance, creating a shallow opening. The hidden depths of this great Lough took on a strategic naval role in two World Wars, when a large number of British naval submarines and warships took refuge here.

Situated right at the heart of the Peninsula Slieve Sneacht (2019 feet) is composed of Dalradian quartzite. It overlooks the rocky outcrops of the King and Queen of the Mintiaghs which stand like sentinels on guard. Composed of a different kind of rock, called "Metadolerites" or more commonly "greenstone", they have withstood the assaults of erosion, retaining their dignity and blocking any further glacial movement across the Peninsula. Bare and awesome they stand overlooking the heather, lakes and bogland all around. The landscape resembles a patchwork, with blue lakes alternating with strips of green pasture carefully wrestled from the elements. Large areas remain uninhabited but as the coast gets closer housing clusters appear dotted across the hillside, the famous homes of Donegal renowned in story and song.

Overlooking the Foyle basin, the rolling pate of the Scalp seems more sympathetic, but the grits and slates that abound create a terrain that is not very hospitable for man. Further inland, access is possible from Ture to Buncrana through Gráinne's Gap with its ominous witch keeping a watchful eye through the Millennia. The landscape changes again with the presence of large quantities of limestone outside Culdaff. It is easily eroded and is quarried for local use in farming, roadmaking and home construction. A fault line that runs from Culdaff Bay to Trawbreaga carries a modern roadway that slices the peninsula in two. Concealed beneath a thin veil of turf and soil, lies the sandy pebbles and gravel of a raised beach, a firm reminder that in pre-history tidal waters flowed where today there is a thoroughfare.

Looking at the coastline beyond Culdaff, jagged rocks dominate with a few raised beaches allowing fishermen the opportunity to secure their boats and their livelihood. As a result of glaciation, strange upright sea-stacks tower out of the water just beyond Culdaff Bay.

Malin Head itself is made of Dalradian quartzite and the area around Culoort has an infinite variety of pebbles and rounded stones, interspersed with gemstones such as Amethyst, Opal and Jasper. The rock formations of Malin Head were fashioned by the thundering powers of the Atlantic and spectacular geological sights such as "Hell's Hole" are aptly named. As if cast off like the black sheep of the family, the island of Inistrahull, six miles away, has a totally different rock formation. Several investigations have shown that the rock of the island is the oldest known rock in the British Isles; it is closer in structure to the rock formation [Lewisian gneiss] on the Island of Lewis on the Scottish Hebrides. Inistrahull is in fact cut off from Malin Head by a submarine valley that relates to the Great Glen Fault of Scotland. From the mainland, it has the appearance of a remote unwelcoming monster rising from the waves, but it has a gentle side, with several acres of green grass to support a deer herd, a beautiful shingle beach that is safe for the swimmer and, strangest of all, a deep fresh-water well, six miles out in the Atlantic.

The search for diamonds which is at present being undertaken is a new development in the history of minerals in the Peninsula. It has been known for centuries that minerals such as copper, gold and barite are present. In the nineteenth century in the historic valley of Glentogher, which links Quigley's Point and Carndonagh, there were thriving silver mines. They operated haphazardly until they were finally closed in 1910. Older inhabitants of the valley recall entering the mine shaft for several hundred yards. Their relatives found employment here wheeling barrows of ore to the mine entrance. Traces of the mine sheds remain but the mounds of spoil that were produced no longer exist as they were used to construct the modern roadway through Glentogher. Copper has been found near Cloncha in Culdaff parish and I myself have seen traces of copper present in the limestone quarry at Foden near Carndonagh. Traces of gold have also been recorded in the Glentogher complex. The gold was contained in galena; alluvial gold has also been reported in the Cabry river that runs from Quigley's Point into Lough Foyle. Prospectors have found gold traces in rivers in Mossy Glen and Balleighan.

Among the farmers of past centuries, bogs were regarded almost as a liability; they produced little more than fuel and were despised for their damp inhospitable environment. But in modern times their wild flowers and spagnum mosses have a special importance. Their value has increased greatly with the development of afforestation and rural environmental protection schemes. Their

heathers now blossom and thrive, whereas at one time they were used for roof bedding for house thatch. The great oak tree trunks that protrude above ground are a vivid reminder that in the Inishowen Peninsula the townlands were almost all covered in trees at one time. In his poems written as he left Derry for the last time, Colmcille records how he looked in awe at the heavily tree-clad hillsides that slope down to the Foyle.

Inishowen is rich in plants that thrive in hilly locations. Along the Dunree river, the Irish Spurge can be found and Scottish Lovage grows close to the coasts and can be found on Inistrahull. Some Alpine plants have also been recorded here, such as the Purple Saxifrage and the Alpine Saw-wort. Most of our long established hedgerows are still intact providing a safe habitat for wildlife. The best known plants are the sweet –smelling fuchsia, white and purple heather and the golden flowers of the gorse or whin. Plants have always been highly regarded by farming people, who used them to make dyes, or provide remedies for illnesses and pains. Inishowen provides a secure habitat today for wildlife such as the fox, hare, badger and squirrel. Although the corncrake is now rarely heard, the cuckoo is a regular arrival in late April. Trawbreaga Bay, Lough Foyle and the townlands of Burt attract great numbers of swans which winter here.

Archaeology

Although the amount of archaeological work carried out in the peninsula of Inishowen is limited, evidence of early habitation can be traced to the late Mesolithic era (post 5500 B.C.). It is generally believed that the earliest inhabitants settled along the coast and river estuaries, gradually moving inland. Flints and stone axes have been found by chance in many areas mostly along the coast. The best known site is a post-glacial raised beach at Dunaff Bay in Clonmany parish. Scrapers have been found here but most of the flint discovered is not local and was probably transported by sea to this site from well-established flint-producing districts in Derry and Antrim. Deposits of flint particles suggest that this was a site where flints were polished and sharpened for everyday use. There is no major evidence found to date to suggest that this was an important habitation for the first settlers. No traces of cooking huts have been found. Samples taken from a nearby bog indicate that there was heavy forestation with birch, oak, hazel and pine.

As early inhabitants developed survival skills, they moved slowly inland and made temporary settlements where they engaged in farming. Evidence of farming activity has been traced beneath layers of peat, which have been removed for fuel. Bog-walls have been found at Cara hill in Culdaff parish and in Buncrana. A unique field system has been preserved beneath the bogland. Evidence of habitation has also been found at Cara hill where a fulachta fiadh used for outdoor cooking was discovered in the townland of Kindroyhead. The site has a Standing Stone; a flagged roadway was discovered several years ago and axe-heads and round stone balls have also been located.

Dating from 4500 B.C., in the periods known as the Neolithic and Early Bronze Ages, there are a number of megalithic tombs in the peninsula, which point to a new culture. These new inhabitants were farmers and hunters who built impressive monuments such as Stone Circles, the best known of which can be seen at Bocan near Culdaff and a partially submerged Stone Circle was recently found near Glentogher. A funerary urn was found at Bocan indicating that it may have been a burial place and some markings on one of the upright stones suggest that the site may also have been an astronomical observatory. Pottery was made from local clay which was richly ornamented. Several urns have been discovered in small burial chambers called cists. Examples of such burials have been found at Bredagh Glen near Moville, Muff and in Inch Island. The tomb at Knocknagrena, often referred to as a Cromlech, has an impressive gallery divided into three sections. In the folklore of the area, it is said that a farmer tried to remove it with gelignite when he was draining the land, but when he left the work for a break, the fairies came and removed it.

Nearby at Laraghirrel, there is another tomb called the Druid's Altar known locally as the Temple of Deen. Coincidentally, both tombs and Bocan Stone Circle are within a mile of each other, raising the possibility that this Bronze Age Triangle was an important area for early habitation. The Glentogher Valley has an important group of Wedge-tombs and there is evidence that it was an important settlement where mineral deposits were present. Two of the tombs are partly submerged, one of which is called after the hunted lovers, Diarmaid and Gráinne. Another partly demolished tomb is called " the Dane's house". Close by, a hoard of Viking armlets was found in the 1930's. In Inch Island, the dolmen is known as the "King's Grave". The Isle of Doagh, or the "Isle" as it is called locally, has an impressive collection of archaeological sites, including inscribed rocks, Rock art, and Standing Stones. One of the most unusual is in the townland of Magheranaul, where a holed portal dolmen can be seen. It is said that the giant who lived here used the hole to open and close the door with his fingers. At Drung, three separate cists were discovered together with an awl, a piece of rock crystal and a pygmy cup. The site may have been a cemetery situated overlooking Lough Foyle.

The peninsula has several reminders of its military past, when settlements required protection. Many of the cashels, hill-forts and promontory forts had a defensive function. Ordnance Survey maps frequently record the presence of forts, but many of these have been lost in the landscape. Placenames too are a reminder of fortification, such as Ard an Dun (the hill of the fort) at Glacknadrumman. The fort which was recorded at Tulnaree, Carndonagh can be identified by a number of rough stone mounds. Striking examples of promontory forts are to be seen along the coastline at Ballygorman, Glengad, Linsfort, Redford, Glebe and Carthage. Many of the artificial caves or souterrains have collapsed or are filled in and an Ordnance Survey map is required in order to find them.

The humble Standing Stone is well represented but the number of stones has declined because of its popularity in house construction as a door lintel. Where the soil was shallow, it was often unable to support the stone. The stones may have been used to mark burial sites, local landmarks, important paths or, as one farmer speculated, as scratching posts for cattle! The most impressive stone can be seen at Ardmore near Muff. Because of a collection of small circles which can be seen on the stone, it has been dated to 2000 B.C. At Ballyargus, the pagan and the sacred were united, as the stone was often used as a Mass Rock in Penal times. An unusual combination of stones known as the Stone Row can be seen at Ballymagaraghy, overlooking Tremone Bay. In all, there are over three hundred archaeological sites recorded in the peninsula. Not only do they represent the culture and lifestyle of our earliest settlers, but they also remind us today of pagan worship, of pre-Christian traditions and beliefs and the myths and legends of peoples, who mixed with Kings, Giants and Druids.

Folklore

The folklore of the district is rich and varied. The fairies had their headquarters among the sand dunes of Lagg but they were active in every townland. In the district of Glenagivney, a woman was in the habit of pouring the hot boiling water from the potato pot outside her door, overlooking

Kinnagoe Bay. One afternoon she heard a voice telling her to stop as the hot water was hurting the fairies just below the house.

Poteen-making was of special interest to the fairies. It was necessary to hide it from the authorities but the fairies were always aware of the secret hiding places. Many a poteen-maker returned at night for his brew only to find it had disappeared. The sound of laughter could be heard in the distance; the fairies had their revenge. The fairies demanded respect from the poteen-makers. It was necessary to offer the first glass of poteen to them in order to secure their loyalty. Those who refused to honour this custom found that their work was in vain, or the poteen hunters were closing in.

Young children were considered to be particularly vulnerable and mothers guarded their children carefully. New-born children were most at risk of being replaced by a fairy child or changeling. Many childhood illnesses were blamed on the fairies. There were several customs which could be observed to ward off evil spirits. If a tongs were placed across a cot, it was believed that this would keep the fairies away from the child. Holy water was also believed to have protective powers.

Farmers too held the fairies in awe. They could interfere with seed potatoes and corn and destroy their growth. Milk was essential in the household diet and if a cow went dry, the fairies were said to have "blinked" the cow, leaving the family with no milk. Tales are also told about the fairy "shot". When an animal took ill, it was said that it was due to being "shot" by the fairies. When land was being reclaimed and drained, workers were warned to avoid the fairy tree in the centre of the field; raths too must not be disturbed. Fairies enjoyed the outdoor life and the fairy beds, where they sported on summer's evenings, can be seen above Tremone Bay.

Inishowen also had its sea god and legendary figures. At the mouth of the River Foyle at Shroove, Manannan mac Lir the great sea god was said to reside, holding sailors and fisherman in his power. The white foamy waves generated by the meeting of the Foyle waters with those of the

Atlantic were said to be the steeds of Manannan. Diarmaid and Gráinne sought refuge here as they tried to pursue their love affair in peace. The sites where they rested at night time are recorded.

At the promontory fort of Dunargus, legend has it that a Viking King took up residence and grew corn to feed his army. His arrival may have been connected with several recorded attacks by the Vikings on the north coast. Inishowen is proud of its beautiful treasures. Near Quigley's Point, a hoard of silver bracelets was discovered in the 1930's. It is well known that Viking raids were made using Lough Foyle in the tenth century and the hoard has some connection with the Viking warriors.

A number of bells belonging to monasteries have also survived. One of the most beautiful is the Bell of St. Mura which is highly decorated. Local people believed that water drunk from the bell had a curative power. It was sold by a fisherman to a collector for £6 in 1850 and can now be seen in the Wallace Collection in London. The Bell of St. Boden is retained in Culdaff by the Parish Priest,

and it is occasionally used in church services. It is plain and unornamented.

A good example of eleventh century metalwork is the Bronze Eucharist vase from Fahan monastery which is in the National Museum.

One of the most sacred treasures from Inishowen is the Misach. It is a rectangular wooden box, heavily decorated, which was used to hold a holy book, possibly a calendar of Saints' lives. Records indicate that it was in the care of Donal O'Morrison erenagh of Clonmany, whose role was to preserve the treasures of Colmcille. The name O'Morrison has been associated with several ecclesiastics in the fourteenth and the fifteenth centuries. They had close links with churches in Cloncha, Fahan and Culdaff. The Misach was of special importance in warfare and it was often carried into battle.

The Grianán of Aileach guards the entrance of Inishowen on an 800-ft high hilltop that offers a magnificent panorama of the "Island of Owen" as well as the twin Loughs of Foyle and Swilly.

The original structure dates to the Neolithic or early Bronze Age (2000 B.C.) and consisted of a central 'cashel' or circular fortification with a series of outer earthen ramparts.

Grianán has a long history associated with the northern Uí Néill clan who ruled the Gaelic Kingdom of Aileach, which reached from Tyrone to Donegal and beyond from the 6th to the 12th century.

The name 'Inishowen' means literally 'Island of Owen' and refers to Eoghan one of the sons of 'Niall of the Nine Hostages', High King of Ireland.

Legend has it that St Patrick came to Grianán in the 5th century and baptised Eoghan in the 'holy well' that lies to the rear of the fort and thus in one fell swoop brought the Christian message to the whole of Inishowen.

In the 12th century Grianán was largely destroyed by the invading army of Murtagh O'Brian, King of Munster who ordered each of his soldiers to take a stone from the fort in their sacks so that Grianán would be reduced to a ruin.

By the 19th century the proud Grianán of Aileach was indeed in need of serious repair and the central stone fort was restored to its present state by a local historian Dr. Walter Bernard between 1874-1878.

Today below the site of Grianán at Burt sits the church of St. Aengus, which was voted Ireland's 'building of the century' in a recent poll. The church of St. Aengus is a unique circular design mirroring the image of the Grianán of Aileach itself on the hill above and was designed by the Irish Architect Liam McCormick in 1967. Also on the main Burt to Letterkenny road is the Grianán of Aileach Visitor Centre housed in the old Church of Ireland which tells the story of Grianán from the dawn of history to the present.

Grianán of Aileach

Fahan or in Gaelic 'Fothain' meaning 'sheltered place' is situated on the main Derry to Buncrana road on the banks of Lough Swilly.

Saint Mura who had family links to the O'Neill dynasty and St Colmcille became the first Abbot of this monastic site, which dates to the Early Christian period. Within the grounds of the churchyard stands the famous Cross of Saint Mura which, it is said, marks the grave of St. Mura who died in 645 A.D. and whose feast day is celebrated on March 12th.

The Cross is unusual in that it is carved in slab form and can be accurately dated to the 7th century due to a rare Greek inscription on the edge of the cross which is a version of the 'Lord's Prayer' or 'Gloria' sanctioned in 633 by the Council of Toledo.

Although the monastic settlement was largely abandoned by the 12th century the churchyard has been in use from the 7th century until recent times. The present church ruins within St. Mura's are of a Protestant church dating from the Plantation period. On either side of the entrance, built into the wall of the graveyard, are two interesting stones. To the right a small Greek cross in relief and to the left a large round stone with a central cavity known locally as the 'Wishing Stone'. Local legend has it that if you stretch out your arm before closing your eyes and walk towards the hole in the stone you will get your wish if your hand fits into the centre of the stone.

The old graveyard at Fahan is also interesting in that it has become the last resting place for some notable people. Near the entrance is the tomb of Agnes Jones (d.1868) who served with the famous nurse Florence Nightingale in the Crimea. To the rear lies Midshipman Horatio Nelson who died aged 18 in 1811. He was a nephew of Lord Nelson who himself died at the battle of Trafalgar.

Just beyond the old churchyard of St. Mura in the present Church of Ireland built in 1820 is the grave of the 68 crew members of H.M.S. Laurentic, which sank off the entrance to Lough Swilly in 1917.

The Harland and Wolff built Laurentic carried a cargo of gold worth five million pounds represented by 3,211 ingots of which 3,186 ingots had been recovered from the wreck by 1924.

Fahan Mura

Buncrana or Bun Crannach (Mouth of the river Crana) situated on the Eastern Shore of Lough Swilly is sometimes referred to as the capital of Inishowen and is the largest town in the peninsula.

Towards the shoreline of the Lough where the Crana River emerges is the site of O'Doherty's Keep. The O'Dohertys, rulers of Inishowen up until the Ulster Plantation, also held castles in Inch and Burt. The crown under Sir Arthur Chichester confiscated most of the O'Doherty lands and castles when Sir Cahir O'Doherty sacked Derry and Culmore in open Rebellion during 1608. The forfeit O'Doherty lands were later leased by Chichester to Henry Vaughan.

The fortunes of the Vaughan family became important to the development of Buncrana. During the 18th century Colonel George Vaughan built the present Buncrana Castle near the site of the old O'Doherty Keep in 1718.

Spanning the Crana River at the entrance of the 18th century Vaughan house is the beautiful Castle Bridge built in the Queen Anne style with six arches rising above the river. The Crana River itself is an important salmon and trout fishing river, which is popular with local fishermen.

Near Castle Bridge is a monument to one of the most important figures of the 1798 Rebellion, Theobald Wolfe Tone. On September 16th 1798 Wolfe Tone sailed with Commodore Bompard from the port of Brest with a French fleet of nine ships and 3000 troops with orders to land at Lough Swilly. However the French fleet was engaged by the British navy under Sir John Borlase near Aranmore and Wolfe Tone was captured aboard 'La Hoche'.

Wolfe Tone was taken from the French flagship at Castle Quay Buncrana on November 3rd 1798 and held there until he was recognised and later taken to Dublin for interrogation. On November 18th Wolfe Tone was sentenced to be hanged in Dublin for his part in the 1798 rebellion but before the sentence could be carried out he cut his own throat and died on November 19th 1798.

Coincidentally the French flagship 'La Hoche' was renamed 'H.M.S. Donegal' and fought at the battle of Trafalgar under Lord Nelson whose nephew is buried at Fahan graveyard.

Castle Bridge
BUNCRANA

Dunree, in Gaelic Dun Riogh 'Fort of the King', is an area in the parish of Desertegney on the Lough Swilly coastline eight miles from Buncrana and looking across towards the Fanad Peninsula.

The area has been of strategic importance throughout history as it guards the entrance to Lough Swilly's deep-water port. The Martello Tower at Dunree Head in 1812 was one of a series of fortifications along the Swilly (as well as throughout Ireland as a whole) constructed to counteract the threat of invasion during the Napoleonic Wars. Other fortifications built locally include Neid's Point, Inch Island and Rathmullan.

A company of the Royal Garrison Artillery manned the original fort at Dunree and in 1894. Field Marshal Viscount Wolseley recommended the extension of the fortifications to include a large fortress and long range artillery guns. By 1900 the extension of Dunree had been completed with installation of powerful long-range artillery on the hill above the fort that commanded a range of 20 miles towards the Atlantic.

It was during the First World War (1914-18) however that Dunree Fort and Lough Swilly really became important to the British from a strategic point of view. In 1914 the deep-water port of Scapa Flow in Scotland where the Grand Fleet of Great Britain was anchored was proving to be insecure from German submarine attack and an alternative safe port for the fleet was sought. So on September 18th 1914 the entire British Grand Fleet entered Lough Swilly under the command of Admiral Jellicoe and a boom was placed across Lough Swilly for the duration of WW1 with Dunree playing an important role guarding the approaches to the Lough.

On October 3rd 1938 Dunree fort and Lough Swilly came under the control of the Irish Government and was to prove a contentious issue between De Valera and Churchill in relation to Ireland's neutrality during the Second World War.

After the war Dunree was used as an Irish Army training camp up until its closure in 1986. Today Dunree fort maintains links with its military past and functions as an excellent military museum which is open to the public and traces the history of the fort from 1812 to the present.

Dunree Fort

As we travel from Dunree towards the village of Clonmany the road begins to climb steeply as we approach the Urris Hills that rise in the distance to a height of 1300 feet. Between the Urris Hills is a steep mountain pass that affords spectacular views towards Dunaff Head and Tullagh Point. Here lies Mamore Gap in Gaelic Madhm Mor or 'Great Gap', a place that has a mystical spirit of its own.

At the summit of Mamore is a holy well dedicated to Saint Eigne a local saint who has given his name to the parish of Desertegney nearby.

Beside the well there is a small grotto with a statue of the Virgin Mary where small offerings are left by local people and travellers. On the 15th of August each year the Rosary is said at the site of the holy well.

The Urris hills are also famous locally for Poteen making which in the past has been something of a home industry in the area. Poteen making in Inishowen usually went on in remote areas to avoid the attention of the authorities and poteen was important locally on special occasions such as wakes, weddings and other social gatherings. Indeed Urris in the early part of the 20th century was jokingly referred to as 'The Urris Poteen Republic' when a flu epidemic hit the area and poteen was used for medical purposes.

Below Mamore towards Lenan is an interesting example of the 'rundale system' or old Irish practice of dividing out the land into smaller and smaller strips between family members which inevitably acted as a contributing factor to the twin terrors of Famine and Emigration throughout Ireland.

The Gaelic language was widely used in the Urris region up until the early part of the 20th century and the famous Irish nationalist Sir Roger Casement attended the Gaeltach in Urris in 1904. Casement again returned to Inishowen in 1913 in an effort to organise the Irish Volunteers in the Urris area. When he later tried to ship arms from Germany to aid the Easter Rising of 1916 he was arrested in Co. Kerry and later hanged at Pentonville prison on August 3rd 1916.

Mamore Gap

Binnion Strand which looks towards Suil Point between Mamore and Clonmany is an excellent bathing place popular with both local people and visitors alike. According to tradition there was a monastery located close to Binnion associated with Saint Colmcille and running up Binnion Hill itself is a good example of a 'Famine Wall' which was built as a 'outdoor relief project' during the famine period.

Near Binnion is the area known as Straid where the ruined church has an interesting and colourful history. During the 17th century two brothers named McLaughlin from Inishowen left the Peninsula to travel to France to study for the Catholic priesthood. However while sailing to France they became shipwrecked off the coast of Cornwall and were rescued by a Protestant Cornish family who offered both brothers food and shelter. One of the brothers Peter McLaughlin decided to continue on his travels to France and the priesthood while the second brother Domhnal McLaughlin stayed in Cornwall and began studies to become a Protestant minister. Years later both McLaughlin brothers returned to Clonmany to serve in the same parish as Protestant Rector and Catholic Parish Priest.

Also in the Straid churchyard is the last resting place of Mary O'Neill of Shanes Castle, Co. Antrim whose descendants include Captain Terence O'Neill, Prime Minister of Northern Ireland. She was married to the Reverend Arthur Chichester himself a descendant of Sir Arthur Chichester who had received the forfeited lands of the O'Doherty's of Inishowen.

The village of Clonmany, known locally as 'The Cross', sits at the base of the hills and nearby at Glenevin in Butler's Glen there is a picturesque nature walk which leads to thirty-foot waterfall. Clonmany was the home of Charles McGlinchey a local weaver who recounted stories of rural life in the Mintiaghs area of Clonmany from the time of his Grandfather in the 1780's through his own life which ended in 1954 to a local school master Patrick Kavanagh.

This invaluable statement of local history was later published in a book entitled 'The Last of the Name' with an introduction by Brian Friel. The local stories and customs that Charles McGlinchey handed down are celebrated each year in the form of the 'Charles McGlinchey Summer School' which is usually held in June each year.

Binnion Bay

Ballyliffin is a picturesque village set against the twin Inishowen hills of Crockaughrim and Coolcross looking towards Malin Head and the Atlantic Ocean. The origin of the name Ballyliffin in Gaelic translates as either 'Baile Lia Finn - Finn's Pillar town' or 'Baile Leith Bheann - Town beside the hill'.

In 1948 a 9 hole golf links was created in Ballyliffin which has evolved to become one of the best-kept secrets in Irish golfing circles. The original Old Links course overlooking Pollan Strand has become one of the more testing old fashioned 18 hole links courses and sits adjoining the new 18 hole Glashedy Links (named after Glashedy Island beyond Pollan Strand) which comprises over 7000 yards with championship tees.

Ballyliffin has been described as 'the Durnoch of Ireland' and recently as 'the Ballybunion of the North'. The course at Ballyliffin stretches for 365 acres of rolling duneland and architects Tom Craddock and Pat Ruddy designed the new Glashedy Links.

In 1993 the world famous golfer Nick Faldo played at Ballyliffin and was amazed at the unique almost lunar landscape of the hillocks and dunes, Faldo was reported to have asked "do you play bump and run here, or do you just run and bump?".

Some of Ballyliffin's holes are spectacular and have a history of their own such as the 5th hole on the Old Links known locally as 'The Tank'.

Today the golf course boasts a brand new club house that was officially opened in September 2000 adding another dimension to a club that has the distinction of being Irelands most northerly course.

Ballyliffin Golf Course

Looking toward Malin Head from the Isle of Doagh the outline of the rock formation known locally as the 'Five Fingers' can be seen punching into the mouth of Trawbreaga Bay sitting below the highland of Knockamany.

The Isle of Doagh itself is situated at the northern end of Pollan Bay and is unusual in that it is not actually an island but rather a small peninsula jutting into Trawbreaga Bay and joined to the mainland by a sandy causeway. This area is an interesting geological example of 'calcretes' where large areas of sand and shell have become 'calcreted' by wind, sun and rain. Also among the dunes and sand hills lie large numbers of prehistoric kitchen middens.

Towards the centre of the Isle of Doagh lies an unusual stone called 'The Mass Stone' which is inscribed with a series of unusual markings.

While most mass rocks refer to the period when the Penal laws were active in Ireland the 'Mass Stone' at Doagh would seem to date much earlier and it has been suggested that the unusual markings commemorate a battle fought by local chieftains. The Isle of Doagh mass stone has been compared to the Clonfinloch stone in Co. Offaly, which has a series of incised markings that have possible connections with prehistoric Spanish engravings.

Near Carrowreagh is another site relating to the Penal period known as the Penal Altar where it is said that a local friar called O'Doherty celebrated Mass in the area during the 1770's.

There is a great tradition locally on the Isle of Doagh relating to the existence of 'Fairies' and the writer Maghtochair claimed that the land around the Isle of Doagh and Trawbreaga Bay was "regarded time out of mind as fairy or gentle ground" and was ruled by the fairy king 'Niall-Na-Brega' (Neil of the Heights).

Towards the road to Carndonagh is the Doagh visitor centre, a small outdoor museum that relates the stories, customs and traditions of the local area from life in the Famine period to the present.

The Five Fingers
FROM DOAGH

Carrickabraghy Castle stands on a commanding outcrop of rock at the North West tip of the Isle of Doagh, looking towards the Atlantic seaboard.

The castle is mentioned in the Annals of the Four Masters and is attributed to the McFaul family between the 9th to the 12th century. However it is more commonly associated with the O'Doherty family who held many castles all over Inishowen including those at Burt, Inch and O'Doherty's Keep at Buncrana. The present castle was built in the 16th century by Phelemy Brasleigh O'Doherty and Phillips' Map of 1690 shows Carrickabraghy as a square keep surrounded by seven round towers and bawn.

In 1607 Carrickabraghy was chosen by the infamous Sir Cahir O'Doherty as a safe place to plan the revolt that would end in the forfeiture of all the O'Doherty lands in Inishowen. The O'Dohertys had ruled the Inishowen peninsula for several centuries until, on the 18th of April 1608, Sir Cahir O'Doherty rose up against George Paulett the vice-provost of Derry City, sacking Culmore and Derry in open revolt.

As a result of Sir Cahir's actions, and the total failure of his rebellion, the government confiscated the barony of Inishowen with the exception of some lands belonging to Fahan Abbey. The English Lord Deputy of Ireland, Sir Arthur Chichester, offered a reward of 5000 marks for Sir Cahir's head and on the 18th of July 1608, while encamped at Doon Rock near Kilmacrennan, Co. Donegal, Sir Cahir was killed by a musket shot while engaged in a skirmish with the English forces. The body of Sir Cahir O'Doherty was quartered near Derry and his head was sent to Dublin to be publicly exhibited.

Thus ended the rule of the great O'Doherty clan and the last Gaelic ruling house in Inishowen.

Carrickabraghy Castle
ISLE OF DOAGH

Carndonagh, in Gaelic Carn Domhnaigh or 'Cairn of Donagh', is a thriving market town situated in the centre of the Inishowen Peninsula and has a long tradition of agriculture and Fairs and is also the site of the famous 8th century Donagh Cross.

The annual Inishowen Agricultural Society's Show is held in Carndonagh and is where farmers and exhibitors from all over Inishowen and beyond show their animals and livestock.

Standing in the heart of Carn (as the town is locally known) is the Church of the Sacred Heart, built between 1942 and 1945 at a cost of £100,000. This church is the largest ecclesiastical building in the peninsula seating up to 1500 people. On the dome stand four statues designed by Albert Power R.H.A. and carved from Dublin granite. The Church of the Sacred Heart sits on a commanding site and its dome can be seen for some miles beyond Carndonagh.

Near Carndonagh Community School (one of the largest Secondary schools in Ireland) is the Protestant Church whose belfry is said to house a bell taken from the 'Trinidad Valencera' one of the ships of the Spanish Armada which sank off the Inishowen coast at Kinnagoe Bay in 1588.

On the main road to Quigley's Point at the bottom of Chapel street is the Colgan Hall, a local Parish Temperance Hall named after John Colgan a renowned scholar and member of one of the chief families of Inishowen.

He was born in 1592 at Priestown near Carndonagh and studied in Glasgow before being ordained into the priesthood in 1618. He later joined the Franciscan Order at Louvain in 1620.

Colgan was indeed a scholar of note and between 1645 and his death in 1658 he published a series of works on the lives of the Irish Saints including 'Acta Sanctorum Hiberniae' in 1645, 'Trias Thaumaturgia' a work on the lives of Patrick, Colmcille and Brigid in 1647 and a volume on 'John Dun Soctus' in 1655. Up until his retirement due to ill health in 1651 he held the influential position of Commissary of the Franciscan Colleges of Louvain, Vielum and Prague.

Church of the Sacred Heart & Colgan Hall
CARNDONAGH

As we travel from Carndonagh along the shores of Trawbreaga Bay we reach the beautiful village of Malin or as it is called locally Malin Town.

The approach to Malin has an impressive 10 arch bridge, which spans the mouth of the Ballyboe River as it flows into Trawbreaga Bay at Moanrealtagh Point. Once across the bridge the traveller is greeted by a 17th century Plantation village with an attractive village green, triangular in shape, that sits at the heart of Malin and is planted with sycamore, cherry and lime trees. The unspoilt beauty of Malin has been honoured nationally by the Bord Failte's National 'Tidy Towns Competition', which voted Malin as the best kept town in all Ireland. This was not the first time that national recognition had come to Malin. William McArthur who was born in Malin in 1809 became Lord Mayor of Dublin in 1880.

The village itself is associated with the Harvey family who under the list of principal landholders in Inishowen dated 1878 held 10,363 acres of land in and around the Malin area and resided at Malin Hall. The Hall was built in 1758 however, it is believed that the present house was built on top of earlier 17th century cellars that may have been part of the manor of Sir Arthur Chichester. Also within the grounds of Malin Hall is the site of a chamber tomb dating from the prehistoric period.

The Church of Ireland church situated on the edge of the green is a fine building with a battlement tower surrounded by square pinnacles. Both Malin and Malin Head are part of the most northern parish in Ireland. The old parish name for the area was called Cloncha (now Malin Parish) and in the Church of Ireland in Malin is a chalice that originally came from Cloncha Church near Culdaff and bears the inscription "this communion cup belongeth to the parish of Cloncha 1638".

Malin Town

Leaving Malin village and once again travelling along Trawbreaga Bay on the way to Malin Head we reach the area known as Lagg. Lagg is the site of the first Catholic church to built in Inishowen following the abolition of the Penal Laws which had prohibited the practice of religions other than the Church of Ireland or state church.

The Catholic Church at Lagg was erected in 1784 and is believed to house the baptismal font belonging to the 7th century Abbey of Saint Mura in Fahan. The church, which sits on the edge of sandhills below the spectacular Knockamany Bens, has a graveyard to the rear that is divided into two sections. The top section which is for Catholic burials and the lower which is used for Protestant burials: a feature which would seem to be unique in Inishowen.

Also in the area is the Malin Presbyterian Church or Meeting House (situated in the townland of Lagg). It is the most northerly Presbyterian church in Ireland.

This area of Trawbreaga Bay (in Gaelic meaning-Treacherous Strand) has a long history of shipwrecks. In 1602 'The Dove' was beached near Malin. The Dove contained a cargo of stockfish and goods valued at £1,302, a small fortune in 1602. This cargo, along with most of the rest of the ship, was stolen and carried away by the local people of the area.

In 1604 the Captain of 'The Dove' a Dane named Hans Mikkelsen asked for compensation for the loss of his ship and cargo from the High Court of Admiralty in London, claiming that the Irish followers of Sir Cahir O'Doherty "cut the ship up and carried the same off" including it is said the captains fine feather bed.

Lagg Church

From the sandhills of Lagg and the fine stretch of beach known as the Back Strand can be seen in the distance the proud mountain known as the 'monarch' of Inishowen's mountains, Slieve Sneacht.

The surrounding landscape in this area is dominated by Slieve Sneacht which is the Peninsula's highest mountain at 2019 ft. and rises above the neighbouring mountains of Slieve Main 1557 ft. and Slieve Beg 1385 ft.

Slieve Sneacht from the Gaelic 'Snow Mountain' can indeed be capped by a crown of snow periodically during the four seasons and is a popular destination for hikers, walkers and climbers. At the top of the mountain is a holy well known as 'Tobar na Sul' or 'Well of the Eyes'.

The significance of Slieve Sneacht has been celebrated in verse by Alexander Reid when he wrote –

"Slieve Snaght, the mighty monarch,
That wears the royal crown,
Is first to catch your wandering gaze;
He looks in splendour down
Upon the little zone of hills
That guard the Royal sire
And sparkle in the setting sun
Like glittering gems of fire"

The Inishowen mountain chain is part of the 'Dalradian Series' of rock formations running across the Peninsula in wide bands up to three miles wide at certain points. Slieve Sneacht is part of what is known as 'Crana Band' of mountains including Crocknamaddy and Slieve Main situated towards the centre of Inishowen.

The 'Crana Band' is mainly made up from deposits of Quartzite's which are hard rock formations resistant to weathering action, this quartzite band stretches through Culdaff, Carndonagh and across to Buncrana.

The Back Strand
LAGG

There is no doubt about the beauty of Inishowen as one travels from one side of the Peninsula to the other along roads lined with fuchsia hedgerows and great stretches of unspoilt beaches. The term 'Ireland in miniature' seems to fit Inishowen well.

One special feature of the Peninsula is the combination of sky and sea that at certain times of the year makes the natural beauty of Inishowen seems like a mystical place. Looking from Port Caman towards Glashedy Island in the deep evening light gives a dreamlike quality evoking images of Irish mythical places such as 'Tír na nÓg'- the land of the forever young.

During the 19th century, Glashedy Island was a popular hideaway for poteen makers who set up their poteen stills in remote places to avoid the attention of the police and 'Revenue' men. Many of the poteen makers were superstitious and one of the customs that they kept was to throw away the first glass of poteen from the still to appease the 'Fairies' who they believed would protect their still from capture and closure.

In the book 'The Last of the Name' the local weaver Charles McGlinchey recounts a local traditional folksong written in Gaelic about a local friar of the Dominican Order called Brathair na Dumhcha who travelled about Inishowen and enjoyed a 'drop of poteen' -

"In Carrickabraghy I was a hundred times
and through the sandbanks drinking,
Down at the Castles I often lay,
And out on Glashedy Island my voice was sweet.
I was often fishing on Trabreigy and in Rashenny
I often sang.
I swam the sea to the Breidin and hundreds thought
That I was drowned"

In the distance beyond Glashedy Island can be seen the Binnion Hill and Dunaff Head which leads into Lough Swilly.

Port Caman

Eight miles beyond the village of Malin is the wild and beautiful Malin Head. A place that seems to leave the traveller standing on the edge of the world looking outward into the wide expanse of the Atlantic Ocean.

Malin Head is Ireland's most northerly point on the Irish mainland and as such holds a special place in the story of Inishowen. The approach to Malin Head affords magnificent and dramatic views of the coastal scenery along the well signposted 'Atlantic Drive'.

In the distance towards Malin Head can be seen the 19th century Lloyd's Signal Tower built by Lloyds of London to report on passing ships.

There has been a long association between Malin Head and the reporting of the weather. Weather reports that were so important to local and international shipping were first recorded at Malin Head in 1870 and the tradition of weather watching is still important in these parts with the location of the present weather station at Malin Head transmitting information for the Shipping forecasts.

In 1902 the Marconi Company succeeded in sending the first commercial message by wireless from Malin Head to the ship S.S. Lake Ontario thus establishing Malin Head as an important staging post for future trans-Atlantic communication, however the Post Office took over from the Marconi Company in 1910.

There are fine views to be had from Banba's Crown on the Head itself and nearby is a deep chasm called 'Hell's Hole' referring to a narrow channel below where the sea is in constant motion. Also close by is a natural sea arch called the 'Devil's Bridge'.

In the area of Ballygorman near the ruin of Saint Machar's Church is an interesting cave known locally as 'The Wee House of Malin' where it is said that Saint Machar lived. Local legend says that the 'Wee House' can hold any number of people and that it "holds all that goes into it, and the more goes into it, it holds the more". Nearby is the 'Malin Well' or 'St. Moriallagh's Well' where on August 15th a pattern called Malin Well Fair is held.

Malin Head
IRELAND'S MOST NORTHERLY POINT

Looking seaward from Portmore Pier at Malin Head to the wide Atlantic Ocean some six miles in the distance can be seen the island of Inishtrahull with the 'Tor Rocks' of Tor Mór and Tor Beg lying beyond the island itself.

Inishtrahull or in Irish 'Inis Tra Tholl' – meaning 'Isle of Great Strand' is a place of treacherous seas and tides. The island was well chosen as the site to guide shipping safely between Malin Head and Inishtrahull Sound. It was reported that on Saint Patrick's Day March 17th 1813 a light shone for the first time from Inishtrahull Lighthouse and it was to Inishtrahull that the first wireless message was transmitted to, from Malin Head in 1902.

There is a wild beauty that is haunting on days when the sea from Malin Head to Inishtrahull rises and falls with the full power of nature and one gets a feeling of the isolation that generations of lighthouse keepers must have felt while manning Inishtrahull.

D.J. O'Sullivan who lived in Inishowen at Greencastle and died in 1994 spent time as a Lighthouse Keeper on Inishtrahull and wrote a collection of poems entitled 'From Fastnet to Inishtrahull' in which he wrote mainly about nature and the sea. He also wrote a weekly column as a nature correspondent for one of the Irish national newspapers.

By coincidence D.J. O'Sullivan's son Eugene O'Sullivan who also worked on Inishtrahull for a time has the distinction of being 'Irelands Last Lighthouse Keeper' when in 1997 the Baily Lighthouse in Dublin became the last lighthouse in Ireland to be automated. Eugene was the Keeper of the Baily Light.

Inishtrahull

On the east side of the Inishowen Peninsula between Malin and Culdaff Bay is Glengad a wild and untamed place with a rich fishing tradition.

A series of steep cliffs some rising to 800 feet high run between the coastline of Malin Head and Glengad with similar cliff formations continuing towards Inishowen Head. Between Glengad Head and the Garvan Islands towards Inistrahull Sound the coastline is what local seamen refer to as 'steepo' meaning that there are little or no landing spots and the water is deep right up to the inshore rocks.

At Portaleen Pier in Glengad the boats that fish from the pier are usually small trawlers and what are known locally as 'Half-Deckers', which fish for a variety of catch such as Lobster, Crab and Salmon at different times of the year. In days gone by a much older type of fishing vessel called a Drontheim was used in Inishowen and in the Glengad area. Some Drontheims measured up to 28 feet long with a crew of a half dozen men rowing two abreast on oars up to 18 feet long.

Local tradition records seamen from Glengad and other parts of Inishowen as being of a very superstitious nature and having various customs and beliefs regarding the sea and good luck. Superstitions included when turning a boat for good luck the nose of the boat should always face towards the sun, it was considered bad luck to whistle on a boat or to point at another boat using one finger, also it was considered unlucky to use white stones for ballast.

Times may have changed but many of these old customs still prevail to this day.

Portaleen Harbour
Glengad

Culdaff is a charming picturesque plantation village situated near the coast between Malin and Gleneely built around a tidy village green with a fine beach nearby at Culdaff Bay stretching from Bunagee towards Dunmore Head.

The village is associated with the Young family who owned 7989 acres in the area in 1878 and who lived at Culdaff House, a fine Georgian house, that now functions as an excellent Bed and Breakfast overlooking Culdaff Bay.

Culdaff House has always been a place of hospitality and has had many famous visitors including Lord Lawrence who spent holidays with the Youngs and later married the daughter of Reverend Hamilton the Rector of Culdaff and became Viceroy of India in 1863.

Near Culdaff is a holy well dedicated to Saint Buadan (the patron saint of the parish who became a missionary to Scotland) as well as a large stone in the Culdaff River locally referred to as Saint Buadan's or Bodan's Boat.

Another famous son was the actor Charles Macklin who was born in Gortinaren near Culdaff in 1690 and later moved to London to pursue a career on the stage, becoming one of the most famous actors of his generation. Macklin who was born Cathal MacLochlainn and Catholic soon changed his name and religion and, as well as acting, wrote a series of plays including 'Love a la

Mode', 'The True Born Irishman' and 'The Man of the World'. The most celebrated role that Macklin played is said to be that of Shakespeare's Shylock of which Alexander Pope is reported to say "this is the Jew that Shakespeare drew".

Charles Macklin died in London allegedly having lived to be over 100 years old but his memory is celebrated each year during the Chales Macklin Autumn School an Arts festival which takes place in Culdaff in October with performances of his works.

Culdaff Beach

The 'Temple of Deen' also called the 'Laraghirril Cairn' is a fine example of a 'court-cairn' or prehistoric tomb from the Megalithic period dating to around 2000 B.C. The tomb sited near the top of 'Black Hill' has panoramic views of the surrounding countryside near Bocan on the road that runs from Culdaff to Gleneely and on towards Moville.

The 'Temple of Deen', gets its name from the local townland from the Gaelic 'Dion' meaning, 'Summit' and has 20 large stones laid out roughly forming a forecourt and two chambers. The other local name given to the Temple of Deen is the 'Druids Altar' in reference to its Pagan past. Another reminder may be found nearby at Bocan where there are the remains of a prehistoric stone circle known as 'Bocan Stone Circle'. It was originally a circle of up to thirty stones but sadly there are now only eight stones still standing.

The area of Bocan itself has a fine Catholic Church which has an interesting story relating to the building of the present belfry in 1933. In the 1930's, during the Great Depression, a local priest Father McKenna undertook to build the Bocan belfry largely with the aid of local labour offered in a voluntary capacity. However money was also needed to fund the endeavour and Father McKenna encouraged his parishioners to write to relatives who had emigrated from Bocan and settled in America for donations for the building project.

When months had passed without donations arriving from America, Father McKenna decided to travel to the USA himself to seek the support directly from the Inishowen emigrant community. As Father McKenna sailed up Lough Foyle towards the United States local people lit a fire on top of one of the hills at Ballyharry to show their support for his journey. The Inishowen emigrant community in Boston and New York welcomed Father McKenna and organised a series of fund raising events which enabled Father McKenna to return to Bocan in a few weeks with enough money to complete the building of the Bocan belfry.

Temple of Deen
BOCAN

Journeying on the road from Carndonagh to Quigley's Point and Lough Foyle we come to a place of quiet beauty called Glentogher.

Situated in central Inishowen between the mountains of Slieve Sneacht and Grinlieve, the Glentogher valley has in the past been a local centre for the mining of ore and mineral deposits. The first recorded instance of mining in the area is in 1790 when it was reported that a new silver mine was opened in Glentogher. During the 19th and the early part of the 20th century, the mines in the Glentogher area were worked to produce mineral ore which was exported through Derry to markets throughout Ireland and beyond and was of economic importance for the area.

The main mineral deposits in the area included lead and silver ore and in 1905, Glentogher mines produced 400 tons of lead ore valued at £4800 as well as 2000 ounces of silver ore. A large amount of bog iron ore was also mined in the locality and was usually exported and refined as a source of iron. It was also used for gas purification.

Perhaps thanks to its mining industry Glentogher was an important staging post for the Mail coach route which ran from Derry towards Carndonagh and central Inishowen.

In the Glentogher area there are a number of standing stones as well as a number of Megalithic cairns or tombs, one such structure is a two chambered cairn known locally as 'Diarmaid and Gráinne's Bed'.

Glentogher

On the road from Carndonagh to Moville, just past the village of Gleneely there is a good example of peat or turf bogland, which can be found in abundance throughout Inishowen. There is a wide expanse of turf bog on either side of the main road running down from the hills of Crockavishane, Crockbrack and Crockaulin.

The tradition of "cutting the turf" in Inishowen is a long one whereby families would depend on turf cut from the bogs in summer, for fuel throughout the bleak months of winter. Cutting, footing, stacking and taking home the annual load of turf was also a social event with extended family, neighbours and sometimes even visitors to the area being press ganged into going to the bog or 'the hill' as it was sometimes called locally.

Indeed turf cutting was seen by many as an art in itself and the proper use of the long shaped turf spade required skill and close attention.

Although in the past turf cutting was mainly carried out by hand, today with the advent of technology most of the turf cut in Inishowen is done using machinery producing what is known as 'machine cut' as opposed to 'hand cut' turf sods.

Another feature of the bogland of Inishowen is what is known as bog oak, the remains of the once great oak trees that once covered most of Ireland in the past. The bog oak, which has been preserved for thousands of years in the moist peat below the surface of the bog, is tremendously hard and much sought after by local artists who carve the it into various forms.

However, it is perhaps the thick carpet of dark purple bog heather, which colours the peninsula in late summer that imprints one of the most vivid pictures of wild Inishowen.

Moneydarragh Bog
Gleneely

B etween Culdaff Bay and Kinnagoe Bay sits Tremone the second of the three bays that stretch between Glengad Head and Inishowen Head at the entrance to Lough Foyle.

It was from Tremone Bay in Inishowen that one of the famous 'Young Ireland' leaders Thomas D'Arcy McGee made his escape from the forces of the British crown after the failed rebellion of 1848. Local tradition has it that D'arcy Magee who had a reward of £300 on his head was sheltered by local people in the Ballyharry and Tremone area disguised as a priest and calling himself 'Father John'. From Port a Bhad in Tremone D'Arcy McGee was ferried out by a local pilot to meet a ship called the 'Shamrock', which was making it's way from the port of Derry on the Foyle to Philadelphia in the USA. D'Arcy McGee later travelled on to Canada and rose to become a prominent politician and democrat in the New World.

On the Dunmore side of Tremone is a small inlet called Port Bronach from the Gaelic meaning 'Port of Sorrow' because it is claimed that the waves make a sorrowful sound here as they roll in towards the shore at this spot.

Nearby Tremone in the area known as Lecamy is the site of the 'sweat house' a small drystone building built in a rough beehive pattern with a hole in the roof which is believed to have been used as primitive sauna and is the only example of a 'sweat house' to be found in Inishowen.

The River
TREMONE BAY

On the road from Gleneely to Moville opposite Moyglass bridge is a signpost which directs the traveller towards the area of Glenagivney and Kinnagoe Bay a place of incredible beauty and history. Glenagivney literally translates from Irish as 'Gleann Ui Chaomhanaigh' or Kavanagh's Glen a popular local name.

It is the story of the wreck of the Spanish Armada ship 'La Trinidad Valencera' located at Kinnagoe Bay for which the area is best known.

Although referred to as a 'Spanish Galleon' the 'Trinidad Valencera' was actually a heavily armed Venetian merchant ship requisitioned by the Spanish under protest from her Captain Horatio Doni. Renamed the 'Trinidad Valencera' she was refitted to become, at 1100 tons, the fourth largest Galleon in the Armada with forty-two guns. La Trinidad Valencera took part in heavy fighting in the English Channel and after the defeat of the Spanish Armada in 1588 made her way north to try to escape, via Ireland to Spain.

At Kinnagoe Bay 'La Trinidad Valencera' ran aground and most of the crew and soldiers escaped from the wreck aided by local people from Glenagivney. The survivors numbering 350 officers, sailors and soldiers decided to march towards Antrim to obtain passage to Spain from the MacDonnell clan but this decision was to have dire consequences.

The result of this march was the massacre of most of the crew and soldiers of 'La Trinidad Valencera' near Elagh Castle on the outskirts of Derry by local militia led by Henry and Richard Hovenden. Some of the senior officers of noble blood were interrogated and held for ransom.

In February 20th 1971 a group from The City of Derry Sub-Aqua Club discovered the wreck and, between 1971 and 1983, began to take up a series of bronze cannons and other artefacts. To date, the artefacts of the wreck have been held at the Ulster Museum in Belfast with those from the Girona until a suitable site is found in Derry.

Today the 'Siege Gun' from La Trinidad Valencera is displayed at the entrance to the Tower Museum in Derry where it is planned that all the artefacts will be displayed in a new 'Armada Exhibition' within the near future.

Kinnagoe Bay

The entrance to Lough Foyle has always been an important channel for shipping travelling up and down the Inishowen coastline towards the port of Derry. Whether it was the Immigrant ships of the mid-1800's or the Navy convoys of the Second World War, safe passage to and from the Atlantic into Lough Foyle has always been of vital importance.

It was with this thought in mind that in 1837 two lighthouses were built at the mouth of the Lough near Dunagree Point in the townland of Shroove.

Shroove or Stroove as it is referred to locally comes from the Gaelic 'Struibh Brion' meaning 'Stream of Sorrow' and sits 3 miles north of the village of Greencastle. This area has a long seafaring tradition with some of the local families having served as pilots, safely guiding shipping in the Foyle for generations.

The two lighthouses when originally built consisted of an East and West tower standing at 49ft and 74ft respectively, however in 1870 the west tower was extended bringing it standing to 99ft. In 1961 the old oil-powered lamps were replaced by electricity and the East Tower was closed down. In its heyday Shroove lighthouse was manned by three keepers but with the advent of technology and automation Dunagree like most of the lighthouses of Ireland now only has a caretaker to oversee its upkeep.

Taking the upper road from Shroove lighthouse a narrow turn to the right climbs up to Inishowen Head where the cliff views are truly spectacular looking from Lough Foyle across the Atlantic as far as the Scottish Isles on a clear day. Just beyond Inishowen Head is Portkill – 'Port Cille' in Irish or 'Colmcille's Port'. Local legend tells how Saint Colmcille came ashore here on his way to the Scottish Island of Iona in the 6th century. He acquired fresh water for his journey and climbed the hill above Portkill to have one final look back towards his beloved Derry. He never returned.

On the beach below Portkill is a holy well and a standing stone inscribed with a cross both attributed to Colmcille and there is an annual local pilgrimage held at Portkill in Saint Colmcille's honour on August 15th.

Shroove Lighthouse

Built in 1305 by Richard de Burgo the 'Red Earl of Ulster' Northburg Castle (or as it was also called Newcastle) which stands at the entrance to Lough Foyle is the most northerly Norman castle to have been constructed in Ireland. Situated in the village of Greencastle it was built on a prominent outcrop of rock looking towards Magilligan Point, where the 'Red Earl' held lands, guarding the entrance to Lough Foyle from attacks from Scotland.

The concern about Scottish attacks was justified as by 1316 Northburg had fallen to the forces of Edward Bruce (brother of Robert Bruce, King of Scotland) who later was crowned King of Ireland. However Bruce lost power and by the end of 1316 Northburg was back in possession of the De Burgo family.

The 'Red Earl' was succeeded to the Earldom by his grandson William, the 'Dun' or 'Brown' Earl in 1328 who it is said slowly starved his cousin Walter de Burgo to death at Northburg castle, when he became aware that Walter was threatening his authority in Connaught. This event had two interesting outcomes: firstly William was murdered near Belfast in 1333 on the orders of Walter de Burgo's sister leading to the end of de Burgo and indeed Anglo Norman power in Inishowen and secondly it is believed that the present day coat of arms of Derry City incorporates the story of Northburg in the form of the skeletal figure within the coat of arms representing Walter de Burgo.

The castle later belonged to the O'Doherty's but by 1555 Northburg was largely ruined due to a feud in the O'Donnell clan, which saw a band of Scottish mercenaries under command of Calvagh O'Donnell attack Northburg with a weapon called the 'gunna cam' or 'crooked gun'. By 1610 the castle of Northburg along with the rest of Inishowen passed to Sir Arthur Chichester and although still strategically important by 1700 the great castle of Northburg was a total ruin.

Above the Norman castle in Greencastle is the Napoleonic Martello Tower built in 1810 as a defensive structure against a feared invasion by sea by Napoleon's forces. The Fort at Greencastle was later extended to accommodate a small garrison and now functions as a small hotel overlooking Lough Foyle.

Northburg Castle
GREENCASTLE

Greencastle is a vibrant fishing village some three miles from Moville looking across the narrow mouth of Lough Foyle towards Magilligan Point in Northern Ireland.

The new harbour at Greencastle is the centre of fishing, the main industry in the area and at present the port is the second largest fishing port in County Donegal after Killybegs. Greencastle port also has the largest catch of whitefish landed in Ireland and supports a large fishing fleet of over 100 boats which has a yearly catch of 6 million tons and is home to some of Donegal's largest trawlers.

The long tradition of the sea and fishing is also evident in the marine infrastructure based near the harbour such as net making factories, fishing co-operatives and the nearby National Fishery Training Centre which has the unusual feature of a mock-deck set out on its roof for training purposes.

Overlooking the harbour located in the old Coastguard Station is the Greencastle Maritime Museum which houses a collection of boats, artefacts and memorabilia relating to the maritime past of the area and telling the story of local people and traditions. Opposite the entrance to the Museum is the site of the 'Inishowen Maritime Memorial' erected in 1997 to commemorate the men and women from all over Inishowen who have lost their lives at sea. The Greencastle Maritime Museum

was a finalist in the A.I.B's Better Ireland Award in 1996 and is the proposed site of a new Planetarium, which will be sited in Greencastle to celebrate the new Millennium.

On Greencastle's upper road looking down towards the harbour sits Saint Finian's Church built in 1783 by the remarkable Earl Bishop Fredrick Augustus Hervey who held the simultaneous titles Earl of Bristol and Bishop of Derry and was referred to as "that wicked prelate" by King George the Third. Local custom has it that Bishop Hervey had the entrance of the church built facing towards Lough Foyle so as to view the attending congregation by telescope from his residence at Downhill Castle.

Today Greencastle is a popular resort as well as a busy port and numbers among its residents the international playwright Brian Friel and Nobel Laureate John Hume.

Maritime Museum

GREENCASTLE

The town of Moville is a picturesque resort town on the banks of Lough Foyle which in the past has been a popular holiday destination for visitors from Derry city and beyond. Moville seems to have two Gaelic meanings translating as either 'Bun an Phobail' meaning 'Foot of the Foyle' or ' Magh Bhile' meaning 'Plain of the Ancient Tree'.

In 1768 Samuel Montgomery, a rich merchant who had served as Sheriff of Derry City in 1754 bought the land that the present town of Moville stands upon and proceeded to build 'New Park House' which became the Montgomery family residence in Moville. New Park House was later inherited by Bishop Sir Henry Montgomery, father of Field Marshall Bernard Montgomery or 'Monty'. Monty later became one of the most successful Generals of the Second World War and received the title Viscount Montgomery of Alamein after his famous battle of the same name.

The beautiful park that covers ten acres and runs along the shoreline which is known locally as 'The Green' was a gift from Bishop Montgomery to the people of Moville and as well as a series of fine walks also has a tennis court, play area and pitch and putt course.

Moville also has a long association with shipping along the Foyle with the first Steamboat service between Derry and Moville beginning in 1832 and the development in the 1860s of Moville as a regular point of departure for emigrants on the Anchor Line ships from Derry to America and Canada.

It was from the small pier near the old Anchor Bar in Moville rather than the nearby larger Carrickarory Pier built in 1847 that people who were emigrating from Inishowen were brought out by small local tenders to board the large ships that would take them on to Boston or New York. Some never to see their families or Inishowen ever again.

What is locally believed to be the oldest bridge in Ireland can be seen at Gulladuff House. It has been variously dated to between the 6th and the 12th century with wattle marks visible on the underside of the arch.

Every year in August, Moville has its annual Regatta and famous Sea Angling Festival and in September hosts the Foyle Oyster Festival, a popular local attraction.

The Old Pier
MOVILLE

About a half-mile outside Moville on the main road towards Derry a turn to the right leads to another monastic settlement attributed to Saint Patrick's travels in Inishowen. The winding road climbs hillwards until you reach Cooley graveyard and the remains of an ancient church settlement.

The site dates from the early Christian period 7th century but has also been ascribed as a pre-Christian or Druidic site of worship. In Gaelic, Cooley translates as 'Enclosed Place' or 'Corner' and at the entrance to the graveyard is a simple undecorated 'Cooley Cross' standing some 10 feet high.

The 'Cooley Cross' is curious in that although it has a pierced ring it also has a carved hole at the top, which is rare in High Crosses of this period.

There is a local tradition that if a wish is made and a stone is thrown towards the hole at the top of the cross and goes through then the wish will come true. At the base of the cross is a rough outline of a footprint allegedly that of Saint Patrick.

To the rear of the old graveyard looking down on Lough Foyle and across to Benevenagh is what is called locally the Skull House, a small rectangular building made of stone which, it has been suggested, was used at different times as an oratory and as a mortuary.

The 'Skull House' at Cooley has its own stories of ghosts and has been described by the well known writer Joyce Cary in his book 'A House of Children'. Cary recounted:

"in the hills there was an old graveyard, surrounded by a wall of loosely piled stones. A church or chapel stood beside this lonely place, long disused, but in the yard itself, close to the back wall, there was an ancient building, all of stone, with a stone roof.

By stooping low and looking through an opening about a foot square, in the thick wall, one could see thigh bones and skulls".

The Skull House
COOLEY

On the main road from Moville to Derry between Redcastle and where the road dips before Quigley's Point is the townland of Whitecastle.

Standing at the side of the road are the old gates that lead towards the shoreline and Whitecastle House, a fine 18th century house that once belonged to the estate of the Cary family of Castlecary nearby. The site where Whitecastle House stands was the original site of a small castle belonging to the McLaughlyn clan in the early 1600's.

Although Castlecary house is no longer standing one of the Cary family, Joyce Cary, has left a lasting impression of Inishowen through his books based on the local area around Whitecastle. In the list of principal landowners of Inishowen 1878 Arthur L. Cary of Castlecary is listed as owning 2182 acres of land however when Arthur Joyce Lunel Cary was born at Shipquay Street in Derry the family fortune was already in decline.

After studies in Paris, Edinburgh and Oxford, Joyce Cary became a colonial civil servant in Nigeria and published his first novel 'Aissa Saved' in 1932.

Between 1932 and his death 1957 he became an acclaimed writer with a string of titles to his credit. However two of his books show Cary's real love for Inishowen. They are 'Castle Corner' published in 1938 and 'A House of Children' which was awarded the James Tait Black Memorial Prize in 1941 that evoked summer holidays spent as a child with relatives in the Whitecastle area.

Two of Joyce Cary's books were later made into films 'The Horse's Mouth' one of the Ealing comedies staring Sir Alec Guinness in 1958 and 'Mister Johnson' set in Africa staring Pierce Brosnan in 1990.

On the Moville side of Whitecastle is Redcastle where today the old family home of Captain Ernest Cochrane third son of the 10th Earl of Dundonald is now a fine hotel and golf course. When Captain Cochrane bought the Harvey estate near the Mintiaghs and later married Elizabeth Frances Doherty in 1886 (who inherited over 6000 acres at Redcastle from her father Dr. Richard Doherty), the combined properties became the largest estate in Inishowen.

Whitecastle Gates

On the main road from Quigley's Point to Derry just before Muff there is a signpost pointing to the right towards the area known locally as Iskaheen in the parish of Muff. Iskaheen takes its name from a holy well in the area and translates from the Irish 'Uisge-Chaoin' as 'Pleasant or Clear Water'.

Legend has it that Owen or Eoghan after whom Inishowen is named was supposedly buried in Iskaheen in 465 A.D. at the ancient abbey which is said to date to the 5th century. The Annals of the Four Masters are quoted as saying that – "Eoghain son of Niall dies and his grave is at Uisge Chaoin".

Other legends say that Owen's youngest son whose name was Feval was drowned in the Lough below and his body was carried for burial to Iskaheen which has panoramic views of the surrounding area. It is said that Lough Foyle takes its name from Feval son of Owen.

Also sited near Iskaheen in the townland of Ardmore is a large unusual standing stone known as the 'Ardmore Stone' or 'Ardmore Gallan'.

The Ardmore Stone stands between seven and eight feet high and is roughly rectangular in shape. It is covered with a series of cupmarks and concentric circles and calculated to weigh around six tons. The design features evident on the 'Ardmore Stone' are outstanding and it is rated as one of the best examples of a 'cupping stone' in Ulster and has also been compared to similar designs on standing stones at Kilmichael Glassary and Baluachraig in Argyllshire, Scotland.

Iskaheen is also the site of the 'Morton God' or 'Giant's Stone' a collapsed dolmen from around 1500 B.C. or early Bronze Age which usually marked the burial site of an important chieftain and was also used as a place of worship. The 'Morton God' is said to be the largest stone monument of it's kind in Inishowen.

The Ardmore Stone
Muff

People of Inishowen

Grianán Aileach is one of the most important historic sites in the North West. It is associated with myth and legend, warriors and High Kings. There are several explanations for the name. The word Grianán is clearly associated with the sun and it is used in Irish to denote "a sunny place". "Ail" means a rock, stone or boulder but for a full explanation of "Aileach", it is necessary to explore the legend of how the site first achieved prominence.

Many stories about the origins of placenames can be found in the Dinnsheanchas but there are also references in the twelfth century Book of Leinster and the fifteenth century Book of Lecan.

One of the best known stories gives an account of how a monument came to be built on the site. The Daghda is one of the central characters and he was the chief god of the tribe known as the Tuatha de Danann. He resided at the royal seat of Tara in Co. Meath and he invited Corginn from Connaught to visit him, with his wife, Tethra. She developed a friendship with Aedh (Hugh), son of Daghda. When Corginn learned of the illicit relationship he killed Aedh and went back to Connaught. He was pursued by Daghda who was intent on revenge. The death sentence was demanded for Corginn but Daghda showed mercy towards his friend. He directed that he should be punished instead. Corginn was ordered to carry the body of Aedh on his back and to wander all over Ireland until he could find a stone fit to be raised as a burial monument. The headstone had to be equal in size to that of the body. He found such a stone near Lough Foyle and used it as a burial monument. It is said that he himself died following the interment, uttering the words "Ach, ach" to express his pain. Thus the site was given the name Aileach. In 200 A.D., the site was of such importance that it was recorded on a map devised by the Greek geographer, Ptolemy who gave it the name "Regia".

The documented history began in the fifth century with the building of a cashel by the Northern branch of the Uí Néill family of the Cenel Eoghain. It reached the peak of its power in the twelfth century when it was destroyed by the O'Briens of Munster. Its importance in Irish history is traced to the rise to power of Niall of the Nine Hostages, a warrior King who founded a dynasty that produced Eoghan, who gave his name to Inishowen and St. Colmcille. Eoghan's territory also extended into Co. Tyrone, (the territory of Eoghan). Conall was a brother of Eoghan and his name is recorded in Tírchonaill (the territory of Conall); Inishowen was not included in its territory.

The introduction of Christianity into the peninsula dates from the arrival of St. Patrick at Grianán Aileach, where he baptised Eoghan in a well which is still there today. To secure the support of this powerful ruling family, he promised Eoghan that if he embraced the new religion, he and his descendants would rule the territory forever. He then set out with his followers on a circuit of the peninsula. According to legend, he first attempted to establish a church at Glentogher just outside Carndonagh but was rebuffed by a chieftain called Coelbadius. An alternative site was offered and Patrick established a monastic settlement at Domhnach Mór Magh Tochair (the great church built by St. Patrick above the plain of the causeway). He stayed at Carndonagh for forty days and left a Bishop in his place to oversee the introduction of Christianity. The church, Domhnach, gave its name to the town of Carndonagh. He then proceeded to Carrowmore where, according to tradition, he visited his sister's husband Conas. The latter gave his name to the monastic settlement, Both Chonais, which is today the parish of Bocan. He travelled onwards to Bredagh Glen, just outside Moville. Here he met his three nephews and ordained the son of Ailill to the priesthood. The site can still be seen today and according to local tradition, it is never ploughed. Before crossing the Foyle into Co. Derry, he founded a church at Moville, close to where the skull house stands in Cooley graveyard.

Monastic settlements flourished in the peninsula up to 1101, when the diocesan structure was established. In addition to those mentioned, there was a monastery at Clonmany and Fahan, and many other sites such as hermitages. The ecclesiastical site at Derry was a Cenel Chonaill foundation but the monastery at Fahan, within sight of Aileach, was loyal to Cenel Eoghain. Six stone crosses mark the location of these monasteries. At Carndonagh, there is an eight-century sandstone cross which is regarded as one of the first free-standing monuments of its type in Ireland. The cross of St. Mura at Fahan is inscribed on a slab which also bears an inscription in Greek, a version of the Our Father approved by the Council of Toledo in 633. Two stark crosses stand separated by a roadway at Carrowmore. A beautifully decorated cross with fine carvings based on the parables can be seen at Cloncha, just outside Culdaff. The unadorned cross at Cooley has an unusual hole cut through its shaft. At Shroove Head, there is a stone pillar near the shore, which has a small cross etched on the surface. Nearby is a well dedicated to Colmcille. It is believed he stopped at this spot on his way into exile on Iona, to have a last look at Derry.

Much of the later history of Aileach is concerned with attempts by the Cenel Eoghain to remain supreme; it was not until 789 that they finally established their power. The great ambition of the Cenel Eoghain was to secure the High Kingship of Ireland at Tara in Co. Meath. Their influence is evident from a passage in the Book of Rights, which lists dues to be paid to the King of Aileach when he was not in power as High King of Ireland at Tara. He was entitled to sit by the side of the High King at banquets; he was also empowered to receive from the High King fifty swords, fifty shields, fifty bondsmen and fifty steeds. The King of Cashel paid tribute in the form of drinking horns, steeds and swords in recognition of the supremacy of the King of Aileach.

In the tenth century, the King of Aileach and his soldiers could see the longships of the Vikings sailing up Lough Foyle with their targets set on Aileach. In 939, the Vikings launched an unsuccessful attack on the fort at Grianán. In spite of their warlike reputation however some of them settled near the mouth of the Foyle and they were also attracted by the deep waters of Lough Swilly.

Although their efforts to establish permanent trading settlements were unsuccessful, their presence is recorded in placenames and folklore.

Of the many kings who ruled from Aileach, perhaps the most colourful was Muircheartach Mac Neill, nicknamed "Muircheartach of the Leather Cloaks", because of the battledress worn by his army. He was hoping to become High King and had shown his bravery in defeating the Danes in 941 in Dublin. He decided on a military operation with which he hoped to impress the lesser Kings that he was next in line of succession to Donnchadh, the High King. His plan was to do a tour of Ireland, in a clockwise direction, keeping the sea to his left, with one thousand specially selected soldiers in the middle of Winter. On the way he took hostages; among them was King Sitric, Danish ruler of Dublin. They were marched back to Aileach where they were held for five months. He offered them to the High King as an act of loyalty but Donnchadh spurned the offer. He was forced to retain the hostages at Aileach but before he could establish himself at Tara, he was killed in 943 at Ardee in Co. Louth.

On his military tour of Ireland, he brought with him a man called Cormacan Eigeas, who is described as the chief poet of the North of Ireland. His exploits and the celebrations at Aileach are recorded in a poem which is preserved in the Book of Invasions. According to Cormacan, ten score of cows and two hundred oxen were slaughtered to feed the jubilant army. In a tribute to his leader at the conclusion of the poem, he writes:

"Receive my blessing Nobly, O Son of Niall Glundubh, bright pure, May Tara be possessed by thee, O Prince of the bright Lough Foyle".

By the twelfth century the power of Aileach was coming to an end. The last great holder of the title, Prince of Aileach, was Donal McLaughlin. According to the Annals of the Four Masters in 1088, he led an army into Connaught and took hostages. Then he burned Limerick and plundered Munster. Finally, he attacked the ancient seat of the Kings of Munster at Kincora and took more hostages. It was too much for Murtagh O' Brien, who set out towards Aileach in the year 1101 intent on revenge. He destroyed several churches, including Ardstraw and the monastic settlement at Fahan. Although he defeated Mc Laughlin in battle his thirst for revenge was not satisfied. In a final act of vengeance, he ordered that Aileach should be demolished. To ensure that it would never threaten the peace again, he ordered every soldier to take a stone from the building and carry it back to Limerick with his provisions. With this act of destruction, the supremacy of Aileach was ended. It was not forgotten as during the eighteenth century, Dean Turlough O' Donnell used Grianán as a place of worship. In the 1830's George Petrie and members of the Ordnance Survey team found a cairn of rubble when they called to the site.

It was not until 1874 that a Derryman, Dr. Bernard, started work on a project to restore the fort. The present structure is the result of his efforts and the voluntary labour of local stone masons over a four-year period. In 1904, the Board of Works declared it a national monument.

The name Tírchonaill refers to Co. Donegal, with the exclusion of Inishowen. The O'Donnells were the rulers of Tírchonaill from the thirteenth century to the sixteenth. Inishowen was a disputed territory and the O'Donnells, the O'Neills and the O'Dohertys all believed that the peninsula should be under their control. In the thirteenth century, two major developments shaped the history of the area. The supremacy of the Mc Laughlins came to an end in 1241 and the Normans later made an attempt to extend their influence beyond the Pale. In 1305, Richard de Burgh, the Red Earl, established an important strategic presence at Greencastle and also at Buncrana; however the Norman intrusion was short-lived. The O' Dohertys were in the ascendant and by 1413, Conor O' Doherty had acquired the coveted title, Lord of Inishowen. With the death of Conor in 1440, two lordships were held by the O' Dohertys, one in Ard Midair near Raphoe and the other in Inishowen. The O'Neills and O'Donnells occasionally challenged their authority but by the year 1603, Cathaoir O' Doherty had inherited his father's lands and was "Lord of Inishowen".

Cathaoir is perhaps the best known of the O'Doherty clan. He was young and rebellious. He soon found himself in dispute with the Governor of Derry, George Pawlett. He stormed the city killing the governor and burning the city. Inevitably, Cathaoir was pursued by the authorities and he fled from the safety of the family castle at Elagh, just outside Derry and within sight of Grianán Aileach. On July 5, 1608, he was captured at Kilmacrennan and slain. His lands were seized and granted to Sir Arthur Chichester in 1609. It was some years before all of the O'Doherty possessions were claimed by the crown but the rebellion and subsequent plantation of Inishowen by Chichester marked a major shift in the political and social structure of the area. The old Gaelic order was now in disarray. The earls, O' Neill and O'Donnell set sail from Lough Swilly in despair in what is known in history as the "Flight of the Earls". The title, "Lord of Inishowen" had no longer any real meaning and those who pinned their hopes on the youthful Cathaoir were now leaderless.

Unlike other plantations in the rest of Ulster, Inishowen was not planted with servitors and undertakers. Chichester leased estates to others who acted as middlemen, agents or landlords. It was the beginning of the landlord and tenant system of land ownership that would have repercussions up to modern times. Other members of Chichester's family inherited Inishowen and in 1647, Arthur Chichester, grandson of the original grantee, was created Earl of Donegall. Other titles followed. The Marquis of Donegall transferred his Inishowen property to his daughter who married the Earl of Shaftesbury. In parts of Inishowen today, rents are payable to the Shaftesbury estate for permission to use turbary rights. The bitterly fought land war of the nineteenth century with tenant farmers pitted against landed proprietors came to an end with the passing of a number of Land Acts.

A new administrative structure was set in place in 1584 by Sir John Perrot. He joined the area known as Tírchonaill with the peninsula of Inishowen, to create a new entity called "Donegal". Inishowen became part of the shire or county system as we know it today. Meanwhile, a new social geography was taking shape in the peninsula. The Chichester policy of introducing head tenants or major landowners was in progress. A steady flow of

English and Scottish tenants settled on Inishowen soil and were offered new leases. In general, they favoured the richer farmlands around Burt, Inch, Fahan and Muff, which were within easy reach of the port of Derry. There were times, however, of great stress and anxiety for them, especially during the uprising of 1641, when they feared for their lives. Fortunately, the rebellion had little impact in the peninsula.

Among the first tenants of Chichester were the Harts and Vaughans. Both families were proud of the fact that they were based in Ireland before the plantation. The Harts established themselves at Muff. Like the Vaughans at Buncrana, they built up considerable wealth by promoting both agriculture and industry and also by securing strong family alliances with other landed families such as the Harveys of Malin and the Youngs of Culdaff. A member of the Hart family, General Hart was one of the few landowners to enter Parliament. The Vaughans possessed considerable wealth in Buncrana, owning estates that covered a total of fourteen townlands. George Vaughan promoted agricultural incentives by offering his

tenants prizes for agricultural improvements on their holdings. The origin of the textile industry in the town can be traced to enterprise on the part of the Vaughans, who attempted to set up a linen weaving factory in Buncrana.

In Malin, John Harvey introduced a hosiery business in 1782 to avail of the excellent linen and wool produced in the area around Malin Hall. Unfortunately, this enterprise failed to prosper. There were times, however, when there was something to celebrate. In 1815, news reached Malin of the victory of the allies at Waterloo. In a moment of exuberance, a four year old member of the family was invited to dance on the kitchen table. In his enthusiasm, he knocked chips of wood out of the table. It was shown to visitors at Malin Hall for many years afterwards.

To encourage local industry, landlords promoted flax growing, water power, bleach-greens, and also spinning and weaving. In the 1820's, steam packet services operated on the Foyle, linking Derry with Glasgow and Liverpool opening up new markets for farm products from Inishowen.

The improvements in farm output led to the development of an industry for which Inishowen was to become famous – whisky distilling. There was a very plentiful supply of barley, fresh water and turf, three essential ingredients for the production of illicit whisky, better known as poteen. Excise regulations were also responsible for the growth of poteen making, as distillers disliked paying taxes of any kind. By the early 1800s, the industry was so successful that revenue officials were sent to the peninsula to hunt down the poteen makers. Later, the army had to be brought in to assist, together with local yeomen at Culdaff, Malin, Moville and Buncrana. Both Clonmany and Culdaff had thriving poteen industries. The weaver, Charles McGlinchy, has described how local people put planks across the road in Clonmany when they became aware that revenue police from Derry were about to carry out a raid. The success of the poteen industry created a dilemma for the landlords, who also acted as law enforcers. They met secretly at Muff to draw up a plan to halt the growth of distilling. In some townlands, every second house was a distillery. As law-breakers were caught, brought to court, and fined, there was great hardship among the tenantry. Soon landlords saw the hardship created in some areas when distilling fines were enforced. Tenants found they were unable to pay their rents and this caused alarm among landlords, who saw their income drop rapidly.

One of the landlords who took action was George Young of Culdaff. So great was the hardship among his tenants that he paid the fines for them. He was also active in attempts to suppress poteen-making in the Culdaff district, but without great success. A thriving export trade existed between Culdaff and the Scottish island of Islay. Moville was one of the main centres for the poteen trade. It was sold at the Magilligan and Coleraine markets, and a thriving "barter" economy also existed. The only legal distillery was at Burt but it was unable to compete with the untaxed product. Rev. Edward Chichester of Cloncha wrote a pamphlet in which he attacked the methods used by revenue officers, who frequently seized livestock if fines were unpaid. Strange as it may seen, he was on the side of the tenants. He admitted however that Inishowen whisky, of the illegal variety, was the best of its kind. Poteen making eventually ceased in the peninsula, largely through the efforts of the churches. They promoted temperance and their efforts can be seen in the Temperance Halls in most towns.

The development of an urban network in Inishowen traces its origin to the time of the Plantation, almost four hundred years ago. It was believed that the landlords of the Kingdom should be allowed to hold great tracts of land known as Estates and develop these for their own benefit and profit. The Community would benefit by the development of Fairs and Markets. To make administration easier Inishowen was divided into four Manors, Malin, Greencastle, Buncrana and Aileach. Early in the 1600's patents were issued for Fairs and Markets in Buncrana, Greencastle, Malin and Redcastle, and in other parts of Donegal. Some of the Markets prospered but others went into decline. Everything depended on the local landlord, his business skills and whether he was a resident or an absentee.

In the eighteenth century, Fairs and Markets expanded to other towns and villages. The patent for the Market in Carndonagh was granted to the Bishop of Derry in 1766. The Fair at Malin was established some time later. The Fairs and Markets were essential to the development of commerce. Farmers brought their corn, potatoes, sheep and linen for sale in the marketplaces, and the market-day was the occasion when people from surrounding areas could meet, socialise and exchange news and gossip. Gradually in the nineteenth century, the markets opened up to all kinds of traders, who could supply household needs. Food such as fish became available in season. Oysters, herring, cod and turbot were in great supply. The sound of the fish sellers advertising their goods could be heard above the hustle and bustle of trade. In warm weather, the smell of fish wafted across the Fair. Beggars also frequented the market place, while others sought to earn a few shillings by selling broadsheets with the words of popular songs. In modern times, the business of Fairs declined especially after World War II and farmers formed co-operatives to sell their livestock at centrally located marts. In Inishowen, the success of Fairs and Markets encouraged the setting up of a livestock mart in 1959. The noise of trade in the main street subsided and some welcomed the fact that the absence of Fairs meant that streets were much cleaner. But many still longed for the hustle and bustle of trade on the streets of the town; stacks of bags of corn or potatoes no longer cluttered the thoroughfares. The carts, horses and wicker baskets have gone and one can no longer stand and watch two farmers haggling over the final pound to be paid for a farm animal. No deal could be finalised without payment of the "luckspenny" and no transaction was complete until vendor and buyer slapped the palms of each other's hands.

Trade of a different kind has bitter memories for some members of the older generation. It took place at the Hiring Fair. In the month of November, children and young adults were hired to wealthy farmers to provide labour for the following year. Some were as young as nine years of age. They stood in the Diamond in Carndonagh while farmers walked to and fro to find a well-built youth capable of doing the heavy work on the land. A century ago, the going rate for a full year was five pounds. In return the farmer would look after the worker and provide board and lodgings. Conditions were often primitive but there were also some humane landowners. Hours were long in Summer. If a worker wanted some cash for tobacco or clothing, it was given on loan, to be deducted from the wages at the end of the season. A mother usually accompanied a young child to bargain with the farmer. As the "Sale" was agreed, the young person disappeared from view waving sadly from the back of a farmer's cart.

In the 1830's an Ordnance Survey was carried out and every road, field, house and building was mapped by "Sappers". Around the peninsula, the marks of the sappers can still be seen on bridges and gateposts. As they measured distances from one point to another, they chiselled out marks like webbed feet on keystones. They were assisted by local people who were paid a wage. In most areas they were made welcome and sometimes fell in love with local girls, as in Brian Friel's play "Translations". But others were afraid that the map-making was part of a plan to invade Ireland.

Their work has brought great benefits to us today. They recorded townland names, although in some cases the spelling was incorrect. They provided accurate maps which are used for planning purposes, and the sale of land. They made notes of important buildings, schools, customs, farming, fishing and general occupations, so that today we have a very accurate view of life in the 1830's in Inishowen. At this time a new division was made in the peninsula; it was split into two baronies, Inishowen East and Inishowen West.

One of the key figures in the Ordnance Survey was John O'Donovan a noted antiquary who sent reports to Dublin on treasures he found; he also recorded unusual rituals, family names and customs. In the parish of Clonmany, the survey noted that it was famous for its home-made clothing. There were over one hundred looms for linen, blankets and flannel. Nearly every household had a spinning wheel and yarn was sold to make a living. Flax was also grown. Waistcoats were very common and they were home-made. Among the sports of the time were cock-fighting and hurling; dancing was also popular. On the 8th of June, there

was a custom of visiting St Columb's well and on St John's Eve, bonfires were lit. This custom is one of the few that survives into the present time in every country parish in the peninsula. "Keening" or loud wailing was common at funerals but at this time it was in decline as it was not in favour with the clergy. Irish was spoken and Clonmany had some of the best Gaelic speakers in Ireland.

Nineteenth century history is dominated by the Great Famine, but occasionally there are glimpses of the social activities enjoyed by some sections of the community. The spectacle of the Tiernaleague Hunt was enjoyed by town and country alike as prominent citizens set off with a noisy pack of hounds. The Master of the Hunt was elected by other members and in the 1840s, the position was occupied by Dr. Laird. The chief huntsman was Tommy Turner. After a busy day in the saddle, there was time to celebrate at the Hunt dinner, with a team of servants in attendance.

On a political level, there was an air of expectation. In 1843, thousands marched from the Diamond in Carndonagh to hear Daniel

O'Connell address one of the largest assemblies seen in the peninsula at one of his famous meetings. It was held at Greenhill, half-way between Malin and Carndonagh overlooking Trawbreaga Bay. As the event did not meet the approval of the authorities, troops were drafted in. They were given accommodation in the Workhouse which had just been built and they were the first to occupy the new building.

It was not long, however, before the Workhouse was used for the purpose for which it was planned. The first pauper was registered in October 1843 but within a couple of years, the number of inmates was set to increase. Signs of blight were beginning to appear on the potato crop in some districts of Inishowen. It was not a cause of general alarm as in some areas, the potato crop was normal. This was the case on Inch Island. But the situation in all areas caused great concern in 1846 and reports were filed of great hardship in Moville and Carndonagh. In 1846, Dr. Irvine of Moville wrote to the authorities in February to express his anxiety. In 1847, Rev. Charles Galway, Secretary of Moville Relief Committee, made an appeal for help. He spoke about destitution, a bad fishing season and the total failure of the potato crop in the parish. In Fahan, on the Lough Swilly side of the peninsula, there were similar appeals for help by the Relief Committee. It estimated that up to three thousand people in that parish were suffering great distress from hunger.

Landlords responded to the plight of their tenants by setting up Relief Committees in every parish to collect subscriptions and to seek government aid. In a letter to the Central Relief Committee in Dublin from Colonel Brooke Young of Culdaff, it was estimated that 1,130 people were eligible to work on road-making relief schemes. Only 136 persons however were in fact working on these programmes. The situation in Malin was no better. Road works were started but later abandoned. Various charitable bodies provided some relief for the hungry. The Society of Friends in Dublin sent small amounts of money to Culdaff and Malin to encourage women to engage in knitting and spinning as a means of earning money to buy food. In 1847, the infamous Soup Kitchens made their appearance. "Taking the Soup" was not something that appealed to many people, however destitute. In Clonmany, the Secretary of the Relief Committee rejected an offer of a Soup Kitchen but requested that, instead, a meal depot should be opened in the village to supply food to the poor.

In 1847, Fr. William O'Donnell of Clonmany was granted one ton of rice for distribution. By 1848, however, meal depots were established in Malin, Cockhill, Carndonagh and Clonmany. A thatched cottage outside Carndonagh, known as the "Brachán House" was a centre for distribution (Brachán = porridge). A plaque and replica Famine pot can be seen at the house on the Carndonagh-Malin road. One of the best known reminders of the Famine is the Famine Pot in Maginn Avenue in Buncrana. It was supplied by Dr. Maginn, Bishop of Derry, who can be described as the Famine Bishop. He was a great supporter of the poor but he too became a victim of the Famine and died at an early age in 1849 after a short episcopacy. He is buried in Cockhill cemetery.

The Workhouse at Carndonagh was planned to meet the needs of the entire peninsula. It was built to accommodate 600 paupers but it was rarely fully occupied, except for a brief period in March 1848. It was seen as a place of last resort and conditions were so bad that most people preferred to remain hungry in their own homes. A strict diet was enforced. A grown man was entitled to receive seven ounces of meal for breakfast, seven ounces for dinner and seven ounces for supper. Buttermilk was supplied also. Men were expected to work, mostly in the workhouse yard breaking stones or weaving. Children attended the workhouse school.

With hunger came disease. In 1848, a ship called the "Brutus" docked in Buncrana with people on board who suffered from cholera. Fear spread in the town that the disease would spread to the local community but fortunately, it was kept under control. Typhus was also a dreaded disease at this time.

A fever epidemic did break out in the workhouse and the Board of Guardians were forced to get accommodation for fever patients in houses near the workhouse. At an inquest in Buncrana in 1848, details emerged of how difficult it was for the destitute to get assistance. A woman of eighty called Elizabeth Byrne died of starvation. It was stated at her inquest that she sought help from the Relieving Officer, Charles O'Donnell. He had made inquiries about her means, and learned that she had five hens. He asked her to sell the hens as it would improve her chances of getting help. Apparently, she was given an allowance of meal but before she was able to collect it, she had died of hunger. Along the coast, some families survived by fishing. There was a plentiful supply of corn in the Carndonagh market but much of it was exported to raise money to pay the rent. The price of corn rocketed and it was not possible for poor families to buy it. In the folklore of the area, a story is told about one farmer who hoarded his corn, hoping for prices to rise even higher. When he went to collect it, it had been consumed by rats.

Nearly every family living in Inishowen has a relative abroad. Emigration has been part of the fabric of society for many centuries. The port of Derry offered access to other lands for those wishing to emigrate. Along the coast from Lough Foyle to Malin Head, people have watched ships bringing their friends and neighbours across the Atlantic. The first great wave of emigration from Inishowen took place following the defeat of Cathaoir O'Doherty in 1608. Some prisoners were executed but others were deported, especially males, suitable for military service to fight in the army of Charles IX of Sweden. In the eighteenth century, many Presbyterians joined their co-religionists in the Laggan and went to America. In 1761 an emigrant called William Moore of Fahan sent a letter home extolling the riches of Nova Scotia and encouraging others to join him. The extent of emigration can be judged from the fact that in one issue of the "Londonderry Journal" in 1773, seven ships were advertised for departure to Philadelphia and other ports. William McArthur of Burt arrived in Pennsylvania in 1783. He was given a job as surveyor in the town of Meadville. He entered the political arena and later became senator. He represents one of many emigrants who made a success of their lives abroad.

In the early 1800s, there was a boom in the shipping industry in Derry. Timber was carried from Quebec and from the Miramichi River sawmills in New Brunswick to Derry. It was a simple matter to convert a ship for passenger use for the return voyage. As the demand for emigration grew, agents opened offices in the towns of Inishowen, where intending emigrants could book a passage. Australia was also a popular if far off destination. In 1839, Bernard McCauley, publican and grocer, of Moville arrived in Australia after a journey of 104 days.

Between 1841 and 1851, especially during the Famine, there was a massive exodus to the New World. Two Derry families controlled the shipping trade. The Cookes were engaged mainly in the Canadian timber business while the McCorkells made great profits on the grain run from Baltimore. The port of St. John was a popular destination for many Inishowen people going to Canada or in transit to America.

While those who emigrated to America generally stayed there, a seasonal migration route opened up in the 1880's to Scotland. Large numbers went from Ardmalin and Greencastle for fishing and harvest work. It continued well into the last century to the 1960s; many went from Moville parish for beet harvesting operations, returning home when the harvest was over. A small number of women travelled from Culdaff for potato harvesting in Scotland.

In the Spring of 1882, a total of 6 people emigrated to New York from two townlands. Among them was my grandfather, John Beattie, who worked on the construction of Brooklyn Bridge. He returned to Culdaff parish and raised a family of seven. Typical of many families in the area, five of his children emigrated to America and were employed in the police, fire service and railways. Three remained in America but two returned home in the 1920s.

Many Inishowen families had distinguished service at sea. Among those who worked on the shipping lines were the Gillespies, the McCanns, the McLaughlins and the McGonagles. Pilotage services were also provided by local families.

Many Inishowen emigrants had very successful careers abroad. Among them was Rev. William

Elder (1832-1882) from Norrira near Malin. He became editor of the St. John "Daily Telegraph". Later he entered politics and was elected to the State Legislature of New Brunswick.

In the 1920s, liners called to Moville to collect passengers. They travelled from Derry by tender and were entertained by musicians as they made their sad journey down the Foyle. Before a person emigrated, a party called a "Bottling" was held but such events ceased after World War Two. It was a tradition along the Foyle and the East coast of the peninsula to burn bonfires and emigrants watched the coastline to see their families send a final goodbye. As the ships sailed away from Malin Head, emigrants crowded on board to wave their last goodbyes, with the island of Inistrahull fading in the distance.

In the twentieth century, one of the main political events that had a profound impact on the peninsula was the Treaty of 1921. As a result, Border Customs Posts were established at Muff and Bridgend, creating an economic barrier between Derry City and its hinterland, Inishowen. As part of the Treaty, a Boundary Commission was set up to define the Border. By 1925, it emerged that certain areas of Inishowen were to be conceded to Northern Ireland. They were the electoral areas of Kilderry (Muff), Birdstown, Burt, and Castleforward. As the Commission broke up in disarray, these areas remained in Inishowen, and the Border was not re-drawn.

Following the Treaty, a number of ports known as "The Treaty Ports" were retained by Britain. The Lough Swilly installations were returned to the Irish Government in 1938.

Within the last few years, Border posts have closed down. Programmes funded by the European Union are having a major impact on both sides of the border. The Border Villages Renewal Scheme has regenerated towns such as Moville, Buncrana and Carndonagh.

Brian Friel, the playwright, who lives in Inishowen, draws inspiration for his plays from the heritage and landscape of the Inishowen peninsula. This is evident in the language and themes he uses.

In one of his plays, "The Enemy Within", there is a conversation between Colmcille and a visitor from Inishowen sent to him in Iona. The words of Colmcille convey a message to generate pride and develop confidence in those who love this peninsula.

"You are from the Kingdom of O'Neill all right. Just hold your chin up, you were born between two Loughs, Lough Foyle and Lough Swilly and you are an Inishowen man."

Bibliography

Beattie, Seán, 'Ancient Monuments of Inishowen', Lighthouse Publications, 1992.

Whittrow, J. B., 'Geology and Scenery in Ireland', Pelican, 1978.

Doherty, D., 'Emerged Shorelines of the Malin peninsula, North Donegal' (unpublished thesis), 2000, University of Ulster.

Maghtochair, 'Inishowen, its History, Traditions and Antiquities', Three Candles Printers Ltd., 1985.

Swan, H. P., 'Twixt Foyle and Swilly', Hodges Figgis, Dublin, N/d.

Nolan, W., Ronayne, L., Dunleavy, M. (eds), 'Donegal History and Society', Geography Publications, 1995.

Lacy, B., 'Archaeological Survey of County Donegal', Donegal County Council, 1983.

Swan, H. P., 'Romantic Inishowen', Hodges Figgis, Dublin, 1947.

Bonner, B., 'Our Inis Eoghain Heritage', Pallas Publications, Limerick, 1991.

O'Doherty, Dr., 'Derriana', Gill & Son, Dublin, 1902.

Atherton, David, 'La Trinidad Valencera - The Story of an Armada Wreck', 1996.

Cary, J., 'A House of Children', Everyman Publications, 1995.

Colhoun, M. R., 'The Heritage of Inishowen', North West Archaeological and History Society, 1995.

MacPolin, D., 'The Drontheim, Forgotten Sailing Boat of the North Irish Coast', MacPolin, 1999.

McGlinchey, C., 'The Last of the Name', Blackstaff Press, 1998.

Ruddy, E., 'Rekindling a Dying Heritage', Ruddy, 1999.

Tohill, J. J., 'Donegal, an Exploration', Donegal Democrat, 1985.

Wilson, I., 'Donegal Shipwrecks', Wilson, 1998.

Dear Reader

We hope you have enjoyed this book. It is one of a range of illustrated titles which we publish. Other areas currently featured include:–

Cottage Publications

Strangford Shores	Donegal Highlands
Dundalk & North Louth	Drogheda & the Boyne Valley
Armagh	The Mournes
Belfast	Fermanagh
Antrim, town & country	Omagh
Ballynahinch & The Heart of Down	South Donegal

Cottage Publications
15 Ballyhay Road
Donaghadee, Co. Down
N. Ireland, BT21 0NG

Also available in our 'Illustrated History & Companion' Range are:-

Coleraine and the Causeway Coast	City of Derry
Lisburn	Banbridge
Ballymoney	Holywood

We can also supply prints, individually signed by the artist, of the paintings featured in the above titles as well as many other areas of Ireland.

For the more athletically inclined we can supply the following books from our illustrated walking book series :-

Bernard Davey's Mournes   Tony McAuley's Glens

For more details on these superb publications and to view samples of the paintings they contain, you can visit our web site at **www.cottage-publications.com** or alternatively you can contact us as follows:-

Telephone: +44 (028) 9188 8033   Fax: +44 (028) 9188 8063